WHY WE GO TO THE HOSPITAL

by Rosalyn Clark

BUMBA BOOKS™

LERNER PUBLICATIONS ◆ MINNEAPOLIS

Note to Educators:

Throughout this book, you'll find critical thinking questions. These can be used to engage young readers in thinking critically about the topic and in using the text and photos to do so.

Reader

Lerner Publications Company
A division of Lerner Publishing Group, Inc.
241 First Avenue North
Minneapolis, MN 55401 USA

For reading levels and more information, look up this title at www.lernerbooks.com.

Library of Congress Cataloging-in-Publication Data

Names: Clark, Rosalyn, 1990– author.
Title: Why we go to the hospital / by Rosalyn Clark.
Description: Minneapolis : Lerner Publications, [2018] | Series: Bumba
   books—health matters | Audience: Age 4–7. | Audience: K to grade 3. |
   Includes bibliographical references and index.
Identifiers: LCCN 2017026121| ISBN 9781512482911 (lb) | ISBN 9781541511101
   (pb) | ISBN 9781512483000 (ebk pdf)
Subjects: LCSH: Hospitals—Juvenile literature.
Classification: LCC RA963.5 .C53 2018 | DDC 362.11—dc23

LC record available at https://lccn.loc.gov/2017026121

Manufactured in the United States of America
1 – CG – 12/31/17

LERNER
SOURCE

Expand learning beyond the printed book. Download free, complementary educational resources for this book from our website, www.lerneresource.com.

Table of Contents

Going to the Hospital

Sometimes we get sick.

Sometimes we get hurt.

We go to a hospital.

Hospitals help people heal.

Doctors work in hospitals.

Nurses work in hospitals too.

They help doctors treat people.

Doctors give sick

people medicine.

Medicine helps people

get better.

Nurses give injured

people bandages.

Bandages help heal injuries.

Sometimes people break bones.

Doctors give them casts.

Casts help bones heal.

How do you think casts help broken bones heal?

Hospitals have emergency rooms.

Doctors see people there when they

need help right away.

Some people must stay overnight in hospitals. Nurses and doctors care for them while they stay.

Why might someone stay overnight in a hospital?

Your health is important.

Hospitals help get you back

to good health!

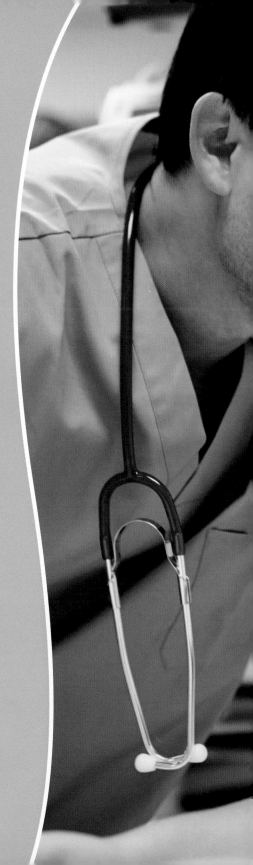

What We See at the Hospital

wheelchair

hospital bed

doctor

nurse

Picture Glossary

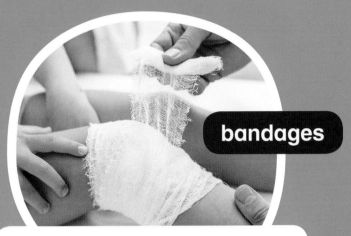

bandages

pieces of cloth or materials that protect injured parts of the body while they heal

casts

hard coverings that hold broken bones in place while they heal

injured

damaged or hurt

medicine

something you take when you are sick

23

Read More

Kenan, Tessa. *Hooray for Doctors!* Minneapolis: Lerner Publications, 2018.

Keogh, Josie. *A Trip to the Hospital.* New York: PowerKids Press, 2013.

Parkes, Elle. *Hooray for Nurses!* Minneapolis: Lerner Publications, 2017.

Index

Photo Credits